LIGHTNING BOLT BOOKS™

Vision: Nearsightedness, Farsightedness, and More

Jennifer Boothroyd

Lerner Publications Company
Minneapolis

For Ava, who looks fabulous in glasses
—J.B.

Lerner Publications Company
A division of Lerner Publishing Group, Inc.
241 First Avenue North
Minneapolis, MN 55401 U.S.A.

Website address: www.lernerbooks.com

Library of Congress Cataloging-in-Publication Data

Boothroyd, Jennifer, 1972—
    Vision : nearsightedness, farsightedness, and more / by Jennifer Boothroyd.
        p.   cm. — (Lightning bolt books™ — What traits are in your genes?)
    Includes index.
    ISBN 978–0–7613–8940–8 (lib. bdg. : alk. paper)
    1. Vision—Juvenile literature. 2. Vision disorders—Juvenile literature. I. Title.
QP475.7.B65 2013
612.8'4—dc23   2011047643

Manufactured in the United States of America
1 — CG — 7/15/12

Table of Contents

Genes

Humans are the same in many ways.

Humans have more in common with one another than they do with dogs and other animals.

But humans also have differences. That's how you can tell one from another.

These team members don't all look alike.

These differences are called traits. Eye color, skin color, and height are a few of our many traits.

Brown eyes and blue eyes are both traits.

We get our traits from our birth parents. Each parent passes on instructions for traits in their genes.

Birth parents are related to their children. Adoptive parents take a child into their family and become his or her parents.

Genes have information about how we grow and develop.

This scientist is studying genes. Genes are too small to see with just our eyes. Genes are inside us.

Vision

One thing that genes give instructions for is vision.

A doctor tests this boy's vision.

People see things that are near them.

People
see things
that are
far away.

11

People
see many
different
colors.

Many genes are responsible for our sight.

Both of your parents gave you genes that control how you see.

13

Nearsightedness

Many people have trouble seeing things far away. Distant objects look blurry.

This girl has trouble seeing distant trees clearly.

But they easily see things up close. This is called nearsightedness.

This boy sees close-up things the best. He doesn't see as well far away.

Nearsighted people see clearly with glasses.

Nearsighted people often wear glasses to help them see far.

16

The lenses are curved to
help their eyes focus on
things farther away.

Some nearsighted people
wear contacts. Contacts are
curved just as glasses are.

Farsightedness

Many people have trouble seeing things close up. Close objects look blurry.

This man sees the newspaper more clearly when he holds it a little bit away from his face.

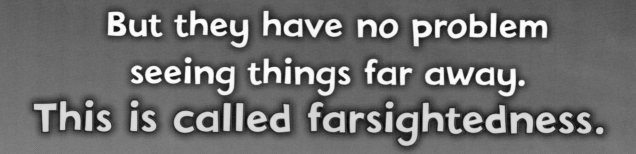

But they have no problem
seeing things far away.
This is called farsightedness.

This farsighted man can see faraway objects well.

Many kids learn they need glasses when they first start school. They find that they can't see clearly when they read and write.

Glasses can help farsighted people see more clearly close up.

20

The lenses are curved to help their eyes focus on objects close to their face.

This farsighted woman wears contacts instead of glasses to help her see close up.

Some people have trouble seeing both near and far. They can wear special glasses to help them see clearly.

Glasses called bifocals help people see both near and far. Special contacts can also help people who have trouble seeing near and far.

Color Blindness

Some people cannot see the difference between colors very well. This is called color blindness.

Someone who is color-blind might have trouble choosing clothes that match.

23

The genes for color blindness are passed on to children from their birth parents.

Boys are more likely to be color-blind than girls are. Color-blind boys usually get the trait from their moms.

Look at these pictures. Can you see the numbers inside the circles? Color-blind people cannot see the numbers.

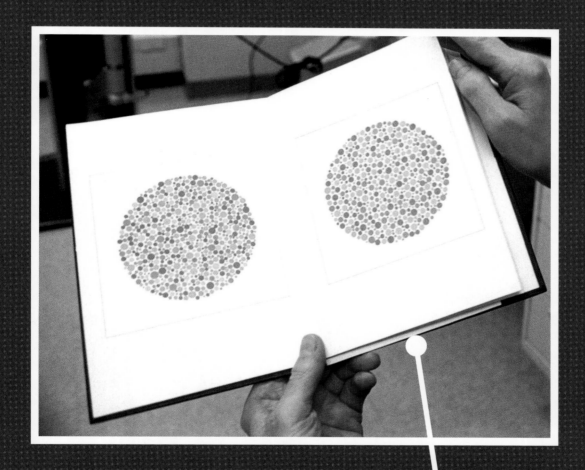

The left circle has the number 7 inside. The right circle has the number 45 inside.

Some color-blind people have the most trouble telling red from green. Others have the most trouble telling yellow from blue.

Color-blind people remember the order of a traffic light, not the colors.

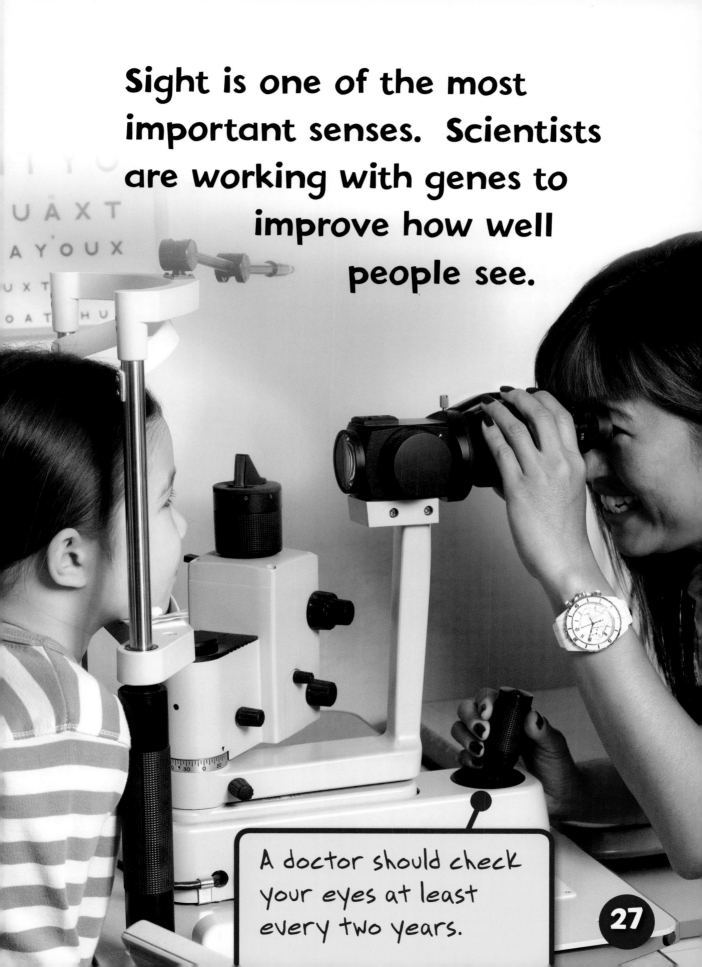

Sight is one of the most important senses. Scientists are working with genes to improve how well people see.

A doctor should check your eyes at least every two years.

27

Activity
Track the Traits!

Track the different vision traits in your classroom. List these traits on a sheet of lined paper:

typical vision (don't need glasses and can see colors)
nearsightedness
farsightedness
color blindness

Then divide your paper into two columns. One column will be for the vision traits. The other column will be for tally marks. (You'll find out what tally marks are and how to use them next.) Your paper should look like the sample sheet on page 29 when you're done.

Put a tally mark next to each vision trait that you have. A tally mark is a straight up-and-down line, like this:

|

Then ask your classmates about their vision. Make a tally mark for each classmate next to his or her vision traits. When you get to five, put a diagonal line through your tally marks, like this:

That's how you write the number five in tally marks. For the number six, make a new tally mark, like this:

When you're done tallying the vision traits, count how many of you have each trait. Which trait got the most tallies?

Sample Sheet:

Vision Traits	Tally Marks
typical vision	
nearsightedness	
farsightedness	
color blindness	

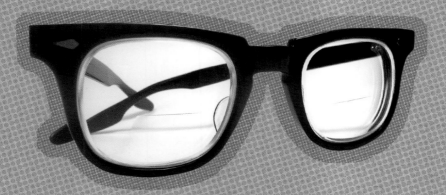

Glossary

birth parent: a parent who is genetically related to his or her child

blurry: out of focus, with no clear outlines

color blindness: a condition in which a person can't see the difference between certain colors

farsightedness: a condition in which close-up objects look blurry

gene: one of the parts of the cells of all living things. Genes are passed from parents to children and determine how you look and the way you grow.

nearsightedness: a condition in which distant objects look blurry

trait: a quality or characteristic that makes one person or thing different from another

vision: the act or power of seeing

Further Reading

American Museum of Natural History: The Gene Scene
http://www.amnh.org/ology/genetics#

Boothroyd, Jennifer. *What Is Sight?* Minneapolis: Lerner Publications Company, 2010.

The Geee! in Genome
http://nature.ca/genome/04/041/041_e.cfm

Harris, Trudy. *Tally Cat Keeps Track*. Minneapolis: Millbrook Press, 2011.

KidsHealth: Glasses and Contact Lenses
http://kidshealth.org/kid/feel_better/things/glasses
.html?tracking=K_RelatedArticle

Index

Photo Acknowledgments

The images in this book are used with the permission of: © Alina Shilzhyavichyute/
Dreamstime.com, p. 1; © Rafael Fernandez/Dreamstime.com, p. 2; © iStockphoto
.com/kali9, p. 4; © iStockphoto.com/Mark Bowden, p. 5; © Laurence Monneret/
StockImage/Getty Images, p. 6; © Shao-chun Wang/Dreamstime.com, p. 7; © Noel
Hendrickson/Blend Images/Getty Images, p. 8; © Ned Frisk/Blend Images/Getty Images,
p. 9; © Inti St Clair/Blend Images/Getty Images, p. 10; © Ashley Jouhar/Cultura/Getty
Images, p. 11; © Paul Kline/Vetta/Getty Images, p. 12; © Peter Cade/Iconica/Getty
Images, p. 13; © Felix Mizioznikov/Dreamstime.com, p. 14; © Ross Anania/Digital
Vision/Getty Images, p. 15; © Jonathan Skow/Stone/Getty Images, p. 16; © age
fotostock/SuperStock, p. 17; © Fuse/Getty Images, p. 18; © Lucidio Studio Inc./First
Light/CORBIS, p. 19; © Chiyo Hoshikawa/a.collectionRF/Getty Images, p. 20;
© iStockphoto.com/jo unruh, p. 21; © Sara Remington/Workbook Stock/Getty Images,
p. 22; © Lenora Gim/The Image Bank/Getty Images, p. 23; © iStockphoto.com/Aldo
Murillo, p. 24; © Frances Roberts/Alamy, p. 25; © 1000 Words/Shutterstock.com, p. 26;
© Peter Dazeley/Photographer's Choice RF/Getty Images, p. 27; © iStockphoto.com/
Paige Foster, p. 30; © J and J Productions/Digital Vision/Getty Images, p. 31.

Front cover: © Tomasz Trojanowski/Shutterstock.com (top right); © KidStock/Blend
Images/Getty Images (top left); © Dmitriy Shironosov/Dreamstime.com (center).

Main body text set in Johann Light 30/36.